FEB 1 1 2004

#55
Playa Vista Branch
6400 Playa Vista Drive
Los Angeles, CA 90094

W9-CPE-918

EVERYDAY SCIENCE

Seasons

To my granddaughter, Megan Kate

Please visit our web site at: www.garethstevens.com
For a free color catalog describing Gareth Stevens Publishing's list of
high-quality books and multimedia programs, call 1-800-542-2595 (USA)
or 1-800-387-3178 (Canada). Gareth Stevens Publishing's fax: (414) 332-3567.

Library of Congress Cataloging-in-Publication Data

Riley, Peter D.
　　Seasons / by Peter Riley. — North American ed.
　　　p. cm. — (Everyday science)
　　Summary: An introduction to some of the characteristics of the four seasons.
　　Includes bibliographical references and index.
　　ISBN 0-8368-3719-3 (lib. bdg.)
　　1. Seasons—Juvenile literature. [1. Seasons.] I. Title.
　QB637.4.R55　2003
　508.2—dc21　　　　　　　　　　　　　　　2003042735

This North American edition first published in 2004 by
Gareth Stevens Publishing
A World Almanac Education Group Company
330 West Olive Street, Suite 100
Milwaukee, Wisconsin 53212 USA

Original text © 2003 by Peter Riley. Images © 2003 by Franklin Watts.
First published in 2003 by Franklin Watts, 96 Leonard Street, London, EC2A 4XD, England.
This U.S. edition copyright © 2004 by Gareth Stevens, Inc.

Series Editor: Sarah Peutrill
Designer: Ian Thompson
Photography: Ray Moller (unless otherwise credited)
Photo Researcher: Diana Morris
Gareth Stevens Editor: Carol Ryback
Gareth Stevens Designer: Melissa Valuch

Picture Credits: (t) top, (b) bottom, (c) center, (l) left, (r) right
Bubbles P. L.: /Geoff du Feu, p. 9(t); /Ian West, p. 16. Ecoscene/Papilio: /Ian Beames, p. 15; /Frank Blackburn, p. 20b;
/Anthony Cooper, p. 10; Peter Currell, p. 24; Sally Morgan, p. 20t; Ken Wilson, front cover (cr), pp.13(t), 21(t), 21(c), 22(t).
FLPA: /Ray Bird, p. 14; /H. D. Brand, p. 12(tr); /Michael Callan, front cover (bl), p. 23(t); /Hugh Clark, p. 25; /J. Watkins, p. 12(c);
/L. West, pp. 18(cr), 23(b); /Terry Whittaker, p. 12(b); /R. Wilmshurst, p. 11; /M. B. Withers, p.12(tl). NHPA: /J & M Bain, front cover (cl),
p.17; /Laurie Campbell, front cover (br), p.18(cl); /G. J. Cambridge, p. 18(t); /David Hosking, p. 13(b); /S & D & K Maslowski, pp. 6, 7.
Photofusion: /Don Gray, p. 8(b).

The original publisher thanks the following children for modeling for this book: Donna Perkin, Nicholas Porter, Ayesah Selway,
Pernell Lamar Simpson.

Printed in Hong Kong

1 2 3 4 5 6 7 8 9 07 06 05 04 03

Seasons

Written by Peter Riley

Gareth Stevens Publishing
A WORLD ALMANAC EDUCATION GROUP COMPANY

About This Book

Everyday Science is designed to encourage children to think about their everyday world in a scientific way, by examining cause and effect through close observation and discussing what they have seen. Here are some tips to help you get the most from **Seasons**.

- This book introduces the basic concepts of seasons and incorporates some of the vocabulary associated with them, such as hibernate and migration, and it prepares children for more advanced learning about the seasons.

- Safety precautions: Many berries are poisonous. Warn children not to pick, handle, or eat them. When you study page 8, discuss skin care and the use of sunblock.

- On pages 11, 13, and 21, children are invited to predict how a living thing changes. Discuss the reasons for any answers they give before turning the page.

- On page 11, expect an answer about the eggs hatching. Children may also mention that the parent birds sit on the eggs to help them hatch. The bird featured on page 11 has a nesting season that starts in May, and the chicks do not hatch until summer. Many other birds start nesting earlier. Their eggs hatch in spring, and the chicks leave the nest before summer. These birds often raise two or three broods of chicks, so eggs may be laid and chicks may hatch throughout spring and summer.

- On page 13, look for an answer about fruit or berries.

- On page 21, look for an answer about buds bursting open and new leaves growing.

- At the beginning of the activity on pages 26 and 27, ask children to make the four tables all at once so they realize it will be a long investigation.

Contents

Four  Seasons

Many parts of the world have four seasons.

spring

summer

autumn

winter

Which season is it now?

Weather

In every season, the weather can change from day to day.

It can be cloudy or rain any day of the year, but summer usually has dry, clear weather.

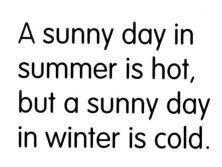

A sunny day in summer is hot, but a sunny day in winter is cold.

It can be windy any time of the year, but the wind usually blows harder in spring and autumn.

It usually snows during winter, but it could snow in early spring and late autumn, too.

What is the weather like today?

Spring

As winter changes to spring, the days grow longer. The weather gets warmer and wetter.

New plants start to grow.

Some new animal life also begins in spring.

Birds make nests and lay eggs.

What do you think happens to the eggs?
Turn the page to find out.

Summer

In summer, some of the eggs hatch.

The chicks learn how to find food. They grow larger and leave the nest.

Other young animals, such as otters, also learn how to find food.

Many plants grow flowers in summer. Insects carry pollen from flower to flower. Pollen helps flowers make fruits and seeds.

What do you think these flowers will change into after the petals drop off? Turn the page to find out.

Autumn

In autumn, the flowers grow
into fruits called berries.

The berries hold seeds, which will
make new plants in spring.

In autumn, some animals prepare for winter.

Squirrels gather food to store and eat during winter.

Winter

In winter, some birds cannot find enough to eat.

Sophie puts food in a birdfeeder.

Do you feed the birds in winter?

Most plants need warmth and light to grow.
In the cold, dark winter, plants stop growing.

Seeds, bulbs, and roots lie in the soil protected from cold weather. They begin to grow shoots as winter ends.

What happens to this plant next? Turn the page to find out.

Plants through the Year

In spring and summer, plants get more light. Warmer weather helps plants grow, too.

In autumn, berries grow, but the leaves die back.

In winter, the roots stay alive in the cold, dark soil.

Tom is setting up a test to see why bulbs grow shoots in the spring.

He puts an onion bulb in a warm place.

After a few days, roots appear.

What do you think happens when he puts an onion bulb in a cold place?

Trees through the Year

Some trees, like the holly tree and the pine tree, keep their leaves all year.

The holly tree has sharp, spiky leaves. In autumn and winter, red holly berries grow.

The pine tree has long, thin leaves that look like needles. Pine seeds grow inside pinecones.

Some trees lose their leaves every year.

In autumn, this tree's leaves turn color and start to fall off.

By winter, all the leaves have fallen.

What do you think happens to this tree in spring? Turn the page to find out.

Change through the Year

In spring, trees grow new leaves. Mild weather and spring rain help new leaves grow faster.

Emily puts a twig that has some buds in a jar of water. She marks the water level.

Find a twig with buds and set up your own jar.
Check the water level every day.
What do you think happens?

Like plants, some animals also change
through the year.

In winter, deer
grow thick fur to
keep warm.

In late spring,
their fur thins out.

In summer, some birds
molt, or lose their old
feathers. Then they
grow new feathers.

Surviving Winter

Just before winter, some birds gather in a group, called a flock.

The flock migrates, or moves, to a warmer place for the winter.

In spring, the flock returns.

Can you name some kinds of birds that migrate?

Some animals hibernate, or fall into
a very deep sleep, for the winter.

This bat has
found a safe
place to
hibernate.

The bat will wake up in spring. It will eat
many insects that hatch in the
warm spring weather.

Weather Record

One year, Harry keeps a record of what the weather is like in each season. For five days during the months of January, April, July, and October, he does three things.

1. He checks the sky for clouds. (Never look at the Sun!)

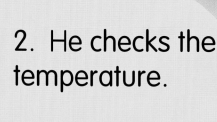

2. He checks the temperature.

3. He measures the rain.

He writes the results in a table.

Month: July		Season: summer	
day	**sky**	**temperature**	**rain**
1	clear	68° F (20° C)	0
2	cloudy	59° F (15° C)	1 inch (2.5 cm)
3			
4			
5			

Make your own set of tables to record the weather in each of the four seasons.

Useful Words

bulbs: balls made by the stem and leaves of some plants. Bulbs grow into new plants.

chicks: newly hatched birds.

eggs: the early forms of animals such as birds and frogs.

fruits: the parts of plants that hold the seeds.

fur: a thick coat of hair.

hibernate: to sleep through the winter.

migrate: to move to a different place when the weather changes with the seasons.

nests: animal homes made from grass, twigs, or mud.

petals: the parts of a flower that are usually colored.

pollen: a yellow powder that helps flowers make seeds.

roots: the parts of plants that grow into the soil to soak up water. Roots help hold plants in place.

seasons: time periods through the year with weather patterns that change with the temperatures.

seeds: the usually tiny parts made by plants that can grow into new plants.

twigs: small, woody stalks at the ends of branches.

shoots: young plants that have just started to grow from seeds.

Some Answers

Here are some answers to the questions asked in this book. If you had different answers, you may be right, too. Talk over your answers with other people and see if you can explain why they are right.

page 9   Your answer depends upon the season and the time of day. You could check the weather in the morning and in the afternoon and compare them.

page 16   If you have a birdfeeder, remember to keep adding more food as the birds eat it. Birds learn to return to places where they found food before and will keep coming back for more. Make sure to place the birdfeeder away from bushes where cats, dogs, or other animals that might eat birds may hide.

page 19   Plants need warmth to grow. Plants in a cold place grow very slowly or not at all. The onion bulb kept in a cold place will grow short roots, or it may not grow any roots at all.

page 22   The level of water in the jar goes down. In a few days, the twig starts to grow leaves. The twig soaks up water and uses it to make new leaf material and to push out the plant parts stored in the buds.

page 24   Flocks of swallows migrate to the south in early autumn and do not return until spring. In late autumn, flocks of geese migrate to the south to find warmer winter feeding grounds. In winter, flocks of starlings migrate to towns and cities for warmth and a regular supply of food. In spring, the flocks of swallows, geese, and starlings migrate north.

For More Information

More Books to Read

- *The Greenwich Guide to the Seasons.*
  The Greenwich Guide to (series) Graham Dolan
  (Heinemann Library)

- *Seasons. Let's Explore* (series)
  Henry Arthur Pluckrose
  (Gareth Stevens)

- *Seasons of the Circle: A Native American Year.*
  Joseph Bruchac
  (Troll/BridgeWater Books)

Web Sites

- BrainPOP: Seasons
  www.brainpop.com/science/weather/seasons

- NASA Kids: Fill-in Puzzle: The Seasons
  kids.msfc.nasa.gov/puzzles/fill%2Din/halloween.asp

Index